Macaroni Penguin

By Edana Eckart

Children's Press®
A Division of Scholastic Inc.
New York / Toronto / London / Auckland / Sydney
Mexico City / New Delhi / Hong Kong
Danbury, Connecticut

Lincoln Elementary   Title 1   Reading

Photo Credits: Cover © Gerard Lacz/Animals Animals; pp. 5, 11, 21 © Wolfgang Kaehler/Corbis; p. 7 © Paul A. Souders/Corbis; p. 9 © W. Perry Conway/Corbis; p. 13 © Grant Dixon/Lonely Planet Images; p. 15 © T. McCann/OSF/Animals Animals; p. 17 © Gerald Kooyman/Animals Animals; p. 19 © Michele Westmorland/Corbis
Contributing Editor: Shira Laskin
Book Design: Christopher Logan

Library of Congress Cataloging-in-Publication Data

Eckart, Edana.
   Macaroni penguin / by Edana Eckart.
   p. cm. — (Animals of the world)
   ISBN 0-516-25054-X (lib. bdg.) — ISBN 0-516-25165-1 (pbk.)
   1. Macaroni penguin — Juvenile literature. I. Title.

QL696.S473E34 2005
598.47—dc22
                                        2004002335

3 4 5 6 7 8 9 10 R 14 13 12 11 10 09 08 07   62

Contents

Macaroni penguins are birds.

They live in cold places.

5

Macaroni penguins have yellow **feathers** on their heads.

Macaroni penguins have a red **bill**.

They also have red eyes.

Macaroni penguins have wings, but they cannot fly.

Macaroni penguins have **webbed feet**.

This helps them swim.

13

Mother Macaroni penguins lay eggs near the water.

The mother and father penguins take turns watching the eggs.

Baby Macaroni penguins are called **chicks**.

They have gray feathers when they are born.

Macaroni penguins eat **squid** and other sea animals.

There are many Macaroni penguins in the world.

It is fun to learn about Macaroni penguins.

21

New Words

bill (**bil**) the hard part at the end of a bird's mouth

chicks (**chiks**) very young birds, such as
Macaroni penguins

feathers (**feth**-urz) the parts of a bird's body that
keep it warm and help it fly

Macaroni penguins (mak-uh-**roh**-nee **pen**-gwinz)
birds with bright yellow feathers on their heads
that live in cold places

squid (**skwid**) a sea animal with a long, soft body
and ten tentacles that swims by squirting water
out of its mouth with great force

webbed feet (**webd feet**) feet with toes that are
connected by a fold of skin, such as those of
certain birds and ducks

To Find Out More

Books
The Life Cycle of a Penguin
by Lisa Trumbauer
Pebble Books

Penguins: From Emperors to Macaronis
by Erin Pembrey Swan
Scholastic Library Publishing

Web Site
KidZone—Penguins
http://www.kidzone.ws/animals/penguins
Learn more about the Macaroni penguin and other
penguins on this Web site.

Index

About the Author
Edana Eckart is a freelance writer. She has written many books about animals.

Reading Consultants
Kris Flynn, Coordinator, Small School District Literacy, The San Diego County Office of Education

Shelly Forys, Certified Reading Recovery Specialist, W.J. Zahnow Elementary School, Waterloo, IL

Paulette Mansell, Certified Reading Recovery Specialist, and Early Literacy Consultant, TX

Lincoln Elementary   Title 1 Reading   E